INSTITUTE OF LEADERSHIP & MANAGEMENT **ilm**

SUPERSERIES

Becoming More Effective

FOURTH EDITION

Pergamon *Flexible* **Learning**

Published for the
Institute of Leadership & Management by

OXFORD   AMSTERDAM   BOSTON   LONDON   NEW YORK   PARIS
SAN DIEGO   SAN FRANCISCO   SINGAPORE   SYDNEY   TOKYO

Pergamon Flexible Learning
An imprint of Elsevier Science
Linacre House, Jordan Hill, Oxford OX2 8DP
200 Wheeler Road, Burlington, MA 01803

First published 1986
Second edition 1991
Third edition 1997
Fourth edition 2003

British Library Cataloguing in Publication Data
A catalogue record for this book is available from the British Library

ISBN 0 7506 5887 8

For information on Pergamon Flexible Learning
visit our website at www.bh.com/pergamonfl

Institute of Leadership & Management
registered office
1 Giltspur Street
London
EC1A 9DD
Telephone 020 7294 3053
www.i-l-m.com
ILM is part of the City & Guilds Group

The views expressed in this work are those of the authors and do
not necessarily reflect those of the Institute of Leadership &
Management or of the publisher

Authors: Deirdre Thackray, Dela Jenkins and Eileen Cadman
Editor: Eileen Cadman
Partly based on previous material by Paul Shanahan
Editorial management: Genesys, www.genesys-consultants.com
Composition by Genesis Typesetting Limited, Rochester, Kent
Printed and bound in Great Britain by MPG Books, Bodmin

Contents

Contents

Workbook introduction

1 ILM Super Series study links

This workbook addresses the issues of *Becoming More Effective*. Should you wish to extend your study to other Super Series workbooks covering related or different subject areas, you will find a comprehensive list at the back of this book.

2 Links to ILM Qualifications

This workbook relates to the following learning outcomes in segments from the ILM Level 3 Introductory Certificate in First Line Management and the Level 3 Certificate in First Line Management.

C1.2   Identifying Self Development Needs
1. Identify requirements of own job role
2. Assess own skills in relation to the job role
3. Obtain feedback on performance and use it constructively
4. Identify relevant development needs
5. Recognize alternative learning styles
6. Take ownership for self development

C1.3   Self Development
  1   Agree development plan with specific, measurable and realistic objectives
  2   Plan to review progress
  3   Implement development activities
  4   Monitor development activities against plan
  5   Revise development plan as necessary to meet objectives

3 Links to S/NVQs in Management

This workbook relates to the following elements of the Management Standards which are used in S/NVQs in Management, as well as a range of other S/NVQs.

C1.1   Develop your own skills to improve your performance

It will also help you to develop the following Personal Competences:

- acting assertively;
- focusing on results;
- managing self.

4 Workbook objectives

Every workbook in the ILM Super Series is designed to make you more effective. So why is there a workbook specifically called *Becoming More Effective*? In all the other workbooks in this series the emphasis is upon you acquiring knowledge and skills that will help you to be more effective in managing resources, change, quality, other people, information, and so on. In this workbook the emphasis is on **you** as the person who has to acquire the knowledge and these skills and then put them to good use in your place of work. How well you can do this depends on how good you are at managing yourself.

Workbook introduction

In this workbook you will look at how you can identify and access development opportunities that will support you in becoming more effective in your job role. This requires you to understand not only what your job requires you to do, but also what skills, knowledge and personal attributes to do it. The workbook will encourage you to honestly assess how well you perform your managerial role, and the information you gather during this process will help you to identify your specific development needs. You will also be given the opportunity to fully evaluate and measure the value of the development opportunities available to you.

In an ever-changing and developing business world all managers need to identify their strengths and their weaknesses, build upon their strengths and convert their weaknesses into strengths. Remaining the same and staying in one place are no longer realistic options.

4.1 Objectives

When you have completed this workbook you will be better able to do the following.

- Analyse and build a sound picture of your current skills, knowledge and personal attributes, using a range of techniques and approaches.
- Undertake a personal training and development needs analysis.
- Develop and revise your own personal development plan.
- Identify and select appropriate training and development opportunities.
- Evaluate and record the training and development activities that you have been involved in.

5 Activity Planner

The following activities require planning and some will take considerable time to complete so you may want to look at these now.

- Activity 2 on page 3 asks you to gather a range of information and detail on your particular job role.
- Activities 6–8 on pages 7–14 take you through a comprehensive analysis of your strengths and weaknesses.
- Activity 9 on page 16 asks you to complete a detailed PESTLE analysis, and where you may need to consult experts to ensure your knowledge is up-to-date.
- Activity 12 on page 21 asks you to offer a copy of the form completed at Activity 11 to at least two different individuals for completion.

Some or all of these activities may provide the basis of evidence for your S/NVQ. All Portfolio Activities are signposted with this icon.

The work-based assignment (on page 71) builds on what you have learned in the course of this workbook. It suggests that you undertake a review of the personal development plan that you have produced while working through the text.

Session A
Assessing your current situation

1 Introduction

This first session will allow you to explore the nature of your job and how you do it. We begin by asking you to examine some of the most basic aspects of it. Why does your job exist at all? What would happen (or not happen) if your job did not exist? We then take you step-by-step through an analysis of the requirements of your job. You'll re-examine your job description to see what you really are expected to do, and then look over the person specification and reflect on which of the skills and attributes listed there you already possess, and which ones you may feel you still need to acquire.

We then move on to look at how you can assess your own performance in your first line management role. What areas are you good at? Where do you think you need to reassess what you do? We introduce you to some common techniques to enable you to look at your areas of strength and weakness, and analyse where opportunities and threats might lie.

Having undertaken a detailed look at your own role and how you perform it, we encourage you to take the results of your analysis to others for their comment and feedback. In this way you'll develop an all-round and – more importantly – objective picture of how you're doing now. This process will enable you to see where you need to take action to develop your skills and knowledge. It will also demonstrate where your strengths are appreciated and where any opportunities for future career developments may be found.

You'll follow up what you find out in Session B, where we'll look at how you can begin to develop areas of weakness into strengths, and threats into opportunities.

2 Analysing the requirements of your job

Each and every job has a particular objective, a reason for its existence within the organisation. Remove that job and something that is essential to the success of the organisation cannot happen. The first activity asks you to think about why your own job exists.

Activity 1

Why is your job necessary to the organisation? What could **not** happen if your job did not exist?

_____

_____

_____

_____

Your answer will depend on precisely what your job is, but you may have linked it up to the jobs of other people, and specified how they depend on you to do what you do to get what they need to be done. For example, unless you issue weekly instructions to your team members, they may not know what they are supposed to be doing. Unless you give feedback to your line manager, he or she may not be able to make longer-term strategic plans.

Every job is made up of **key tasks and activities**. These are the different elements of the job that you perform in order to get the job done. In the examples given in the previous paragraph, two key tasks or activities were described – 'issue weekly instructions to team members' and 'give feedback to my line manager'.

In order to complete these key tasks and activities, the jobholder should:

- possess **skills** relevant to the tasks and activities;
- hold **knowledge** that underpins, or supports these skills;
- possess certain **personal attributes** that are appropriate to the job.

For example, to successfully undertake the key tasks listed above, you would require good communication skills, you would need to know what your team had achieved, and know how to present that information in a suitable form to your line manager. You might also need the personal attributes of approachability and clear-headedness in order to find out that information and present it in a suitable manner.

The next activity gives you the opportunity to explore each of these aspects of your own job.

Activity 2

20 mins

Gather documentation that will supply information on:

■ your actual job role – its key tasks and activities;
■ the skills, knowledge and behaviour essential to fulfilling these tasks and activities.

Make a brief list of the various documents that you have gathered.

_____

_____

_____

_____

_____

Job-related information comes in a range of forms and from a variety of sources. You might have obtained:

■ a job description – that details the practicalities and requirements of the job;
■ a person specification – that sets out the essential and desirable skills, knowledge and personal attributes needed by the jobholder;
■ completed appraisal or performance review forms – that contain information on how the person in the job is carrying out that job;
■ an organisation chart – showing the relationship between your job role and others within the company.

You might also have held discussions with your line manager, human resource staff, colleagues or others doing the same job as you to find out more.

2.1 The key tasks of your job

Activity 3

10 mins

Using the information you have gathered, write down a list of the key tasks and activities that your job requires you to do.

_____

_____

_____

_____

_____

_____

_____

Your answer to this activity will of course depend on the precise nature of your job. The point is that you are clear about what the key tasks actually are.

2.2 The skills, knowledge and personal attributes needed in your job

In order to be effective in doing our particular job, we need a combination of skills, knowledge and personal attributes. These need to support and complement one another. In the previous activity you listed the various tasks you do, all of which will require a different combination of skills, knowledge and personal attributes, in order for the person carrying out the work to be effective.

Activity 4

10 mins

Using the information you gathered in Activity 2, write down a list of the skills, knowledge and personal attributes that you need to possess to do your job.

_____

_____

_____

_____

Again, the answer you give will depend on the nature of your job, but you may have mentioned items as varied as good communication skills, a head for figures or a good memory, sensitivity in dealing with the public, or a disciplined approach to paperwork.

Of course jobs change, and it is often the case that the documentation, for example a job description, is no longer a true reflection of what the job actually involves. Sometimes jobs change because the person doing the job finds it necessary to make changes; new and more effective ways are found of carrying out the necessary tasks or activities; organizational structures change; customer needs and supplier capability change or adapt over time.

If necessary, identify items on the list that you made in the previous activity that may not be up-to-date. You may need to discuss with your line manager or the personnel department how they might be made more relevant to your present situation.

Up until now, we've asked you to look at the requirements of your job overall. Now let's look at what it needs in a bit more detail.

Activity 5 ·

5 mins

Identify **one** key task of your current job, and write a brief description of it.

_____

_____

_____

Now ask yourself the following questions.

■ What do I need to be able to **do** to carry out this key part of my job (skill)?

_____

■ What do I need to **know** to carry out this key part of my job (knowledge)?

_____

■ What personal attributes do I need to **possess** to carry out this part of my job?

_____

There's no right answer here, since it will depend on which task you chose. If you had identified giving presentations as your example, then you might have identified the skill of preparing overhead slides, or handouts. The obvious knowledge in this instance would be the knowledge of the actual subject area, and knowledge of how to present information in a way that can be understood by your audience. The personal attributes might have included having the self-confidence to stand in front of the audience concerned.

Each task required by your job can be analysed in terms of the necessary skills, knowledge and personal attributes needed by the person doing it.

2.3 Assessing your own performance

Having looked at what your job requires, both in terms of its essential tasks and activities, and what it requires of you, we'll now go on to explore how good **you** feel you are at your job. How well do you think you perform on a day-to-day basis? Don't worry! The point about this exercise is not to make you feel that you're falling short in some way. Rather, it's to give you the chance to examine where your own development needs lie. This will not only help you to see how you might do your current job more effectively, but also give your confidence a boost and help you to see how your future career might develop. All managers, even the ones at the top of organizations, need to undertake this sort of assessment at one time or another, so you aren't being asked to do anything out of the ordinary here.

It has probably occurred to you that your own self-assessment may turn out to be a bit biased! In a later activity, we'll ask you to get other colleagues to give their opinion of the results. You might find it useful to begin thinking about who you might approach.

The one thing that's clear about managerial roles is that they are all different. So, how can we possibly go about assessing our performance? What activities do they all have in common that we can use as benchmarks? Although your job may be quite specific in terms of the practical activities you carry out, the role of any manager is likely to include managing:

- activities and quality;
- financial and physical resources;
- other people, yourself and relationships;
- communication and information.

The next activity is designed to help you begin to think about how well you do the tasks required in these four different aspects of your job.

Activity 6

20 mins

Portfolio of evidence

S/NVQ C1.1

This Activity may provide the basis of appropriate evidence for your S/NVQ portfolio. If you are intending to take this course of action it might be better to write your answers on separate sheets of paper.

The following questionnaire will provide you with a preliminary picture of your own effectiveness across these areas of management. The tasks and activities illustrated are by no means a comprehensive listing of all the aspects of management in which you might be involved, but are meant to offer you the opportunity to consider these fundamental areas of your work.

(You may want to look back at the list of key tasks you drew up in Activity 3, to see whether it includes any essential tasks not contained in the questionnaire. If it does, add them to the questionnaire in the spaces provided.)

For each checklist item, ask yourself to what extent you usually achieve either the effects you intended or the outcomes that others (your manager, staff, customers, etc.) expect from you. Give yourself a rating from 1 to 5, where 1 equals 'very poor' and 5 equals 'very good', by circling the appropriate number in the column headed 'How effective are you?'.

Be as honest as you can. However, if you have sufficient time to consult someone else, then you might want to include their input as well. The results of this questionnaire are for your benefit only, and will give a basis for consideration later in this session.

a   Manage activities and quality

Task/Activity	How effective are you?
Agree requirements with internal and/or external customers.	1 – 2 – 3 – 4 – 5
Explain customer requirements to team members and to others both within and outside the organisation.	1 – 2 – 3 – 4 – 5
Plan work activities to meet required objectives.	1 – 2 – 3 – 4 – 5
Identify areas where quality can be improved.	1 – 2 – 3 – 4 – 5
Involve others in making improvements to work activities.	1 – 2 – 3 – 4 – 5
Implement and co-ordinate planned change.	1 – 2 – 3 – 4 – 5
Assess the costs (either increases or savings) associated with change.	1 – 2 – 3 – 4 – 5
Monitor the team's work.	1 – 2 – 3 – 4 – 5
Inform others of their legal and organizational responsibilities in terms of health and safety.	1 – 2 – 3 – 4 – 5
Ensure that working conditions conform to legal and organisational requirements for health, safety and the environment.	1 – 2 – 3 – 4 – 5
	1 – 2 – 3 – 4 – 5

b   Manage financial and physical resources

Tasks/Activities	How effective are you?
Measure your team's performance against agreed objectives.	1 – 2 – 3 – 4 – 5
Monitor performance against budget, and reduce unacceptable variances.	1 – 2 – 3 – 4 – 5
Maintain an effective system for supply, storage and issue of materials for operations.	1 – 2 – 3 – 4 – 5
Plan the activities of team members to achieve work objectives.	1 – 2 – 3 – 4 – 5
Monitor the use of resources.	1 – 2 – 3 – 4 – 5
Identify staffing needs.	1 – 2 – 3 – 4 – 5
Control the use of equipment and maintain it safely, efficiently and effectively.	1 – 2 – 3 – 4 – 5
Ensure the security of personnel, stock, equipment and data in the workplace.	1 – 2 – 3 – 4 – 5
Create and implement action plans to identify and reduce waste.	1 – 2 – 3 – 4 – 5
Maintain complete and accurate records of resource use.	1 – 2 – 3 – 4 – 5
	1 – 2 – 3 – 4 – 5

c   Manage other people, yourself and relationships

Tasks/Activities	How effective are you?
Assess both your own skills and those of your team members to identify development needs.	1 – 2 – 3 – 4 – 5
Create and implement development plans that contain specific, measurable and realistic objectives.	1 – 2 – 3 – 4 – 5
Organize training activities that are consistent with your team development plans.	1 – 2 – 3 – 4 – 5
Build an effective and mutually supportive team.	1 – 2 – 3 – 4 – 5
Recognize symptoms of stress in yourself and your team members, and resolve it effectively.	1 – 2 – 3 – 4 – 5
Manage your team in accordance with the principles of equal opportunity and diversity.	1 – 2 – 3 – 4 – 5
Identify and implement appropriate solutions to problems.	1 – 2 – 3 – 4 – 5
Provide appropriate opportunities for team members to discuss problems.	1 – 2 – 3 – 4 – 5
Use motivation to ensure your team's commitment to change.	1 – 2 – 3 – 4 – 5
Manage time to meet your objectives.	1 – 2 – 3 – 4 – 5
	1 – 2 – 3 – 4 – 5

d   Manage communication and information

Tasks/Activities	How effective are you?
Gather accurate, sufficient and relevant information that is fit for its intended purpose.	1 – 2 – 3 – 4 – 5
Record and store information in ways that are in line with organizational systems and procedures.	1 – 2 – 3 – 4 – 5
Present information at a time and place, and in a form and manner appropriate to the intended recipients.	1 – 2 – 3 – 4 – 5
Obtain and give feedback, and use it to enhance performance.	1 – 2 – 3 – 4 – 5
Lead meetings in a way that helps people to make useful contributions, and which discourages unhelpful arguments and digressions.	1 – 2 – 3 – 4 – 5
Gain the trust and support of your line manager, colleagues and team members.	1 – 2 – 3 – 4 – 5
Collect verbal and non-verbal data and use it to interpret and monitor the attitudes of others.	1 – 2 – 3 – 4 – 5
Use networking as a tool to manage more effectively.	1 – 2 – 3 – 4 – 5
Use negotiation to resolve conflict.	1 – 2 – 3 – 4 – 5
Keep accurate, confidential records of conflicts and their outcomes.	1 – 2 – 3 – 4 – 5
	1 – 2 – 3 – 4 – 5

When you have completed the questionnaire, work out your average rating for each of the four areas of management. Do this by adding up the scores of all the relevant activities that you circled and divide by the number of relevant activities in that area. (For example, if you only circled four of the activities in 'Manage activities and quality', then add those scores together and divide by four.)

Put your four averages in the table below.

Managing activities and quality:	Managing financial and physical resources:
Managing other people, yourself and relationships:	Managing communication and information:

The results you obtain will show you which management areas you are good at, and which are likely ones for further development. For example, you might find that you scored a high average for managing resources, but less highly on managing people.

3 Assessing your current effectiveness

Each of us has strengths as well as weaknesses. We work well in particular situations, less well in others – often we feel stronger when we are carrying out tasks that we enjoy; the response from others is more likely to be positive and we actively seek out similar situations so that we can get this positive response. The opposite then can also be true – where we get a less positive response we actively avoid putting ourselves in the same situation. The result is that we build on positive and strong performance, but avoid situations where we display our weakness.

3.1 Reviewing your strengths and weaknesses

The remainder of this workbook is mainly concerned with planning ways of developing the skills and task areas in which you are weakest. For now, it might be useful to think about this a bit more by summarizing those skills and task areas in which you are particularly strong, and prioritizing those that you think need most attention.

Remember to ask yourself the following the key questions.

■   What do I need to be able to do?
■   What do I need to know?
■   What personal attributes do I need?

Activity 7 · 10 mins

S/NVQ C1.1

This Activity may provide the basis of appropriate evidence for your S/NVQ portfolio. If you are intending to take this course of action it might be better to write your answers on separate sheets of paper.

Look back at Activity 6 and, for each area of management activity, make a list of the skills or tasks in which you are particularly strong. Ask yourself these questions. What are my strengths? What am I good at? Where do I get positive results?

Managing activities and quality

_____

_____

_____

_____

_____

Managing financial and physical resources

_____

_____

_____

_____

_____

Managing other people, yourself and relationships

_____

_____

_____

_____

_____

Managing communication and information

_____

_____

_____

_____

_____

You may have found that, on consideration, you have certain strengths which you always took for granted. You may also have found that, on reflection, you are not as strong as you thought you were.

Activity 8

10 mins

S/NVQ C1.1

This Activity may provide the basis of appropriate evidence for your S/NVQ portfolio. If you are intending to take this course of action it might be better to write your answers on separate sheets of paper.

Now consider those areas in Activity 6 in which you consider yourself particularly weak. Again, list them according to management area, but this time give your reason (perhaps an example) to show why you think you are weak.

Area of weakness	My reason for thinking I am weak in this area is . . .
Managing activities and quality	
Managing financial and physical resources	
Managing other people, yourself and relationships	
Managing communication and information	

You should now have a comprehensive listing of all your main areas of strength and weakness. This will form the basis of much of your work in the rest of the workbook.

3.2 PESTLE analysis

A PESTLE analysis is a further approach that you can use to gauge your current and future effectiveness. You need to consider a variety of factors that will affect you and your organization. These factors are as follows.

- **P**olitical
- **E**conomic
- **S**ocial
- **T**echnological
- **L**egal
- **E**nvironmental/ecological

Political factors

The government affects the ways in which a business can operate, usually through the legal and regulatory controls that it applies. In the twenty-first century businesses will need to face a range of political issues, for example relationships with overseas markets, development of transport systems, and world security issues.

Economic factors

Availability of money through an increased number of customers, or increased costs from suppliers will directly affect the business. At the same time changes to interest rates and inflationary effects will also have an impact upon how the business operates. Rates of exchange will also affect businesses that have dealings with customers or suppliers outside the UK. Stock market values may be another crucial factor.

Social factors

Organizations are affected by the availability of skilled and qualified staff, as well as the age and gender of the population from which it draws its staff. Issues such as child-care, or the care of elderly parents will affect working practices. Changing spending patterns and overall attitudes to careers will also have an impact on how the business operates and makes decisions.

Technological factors

As complex technology becomes more accessible, the methods and speed of communication will develop. Organizations can process and exchange information quickly, both within the business and in relation to its customers and suppliers. Organizations may face the need to keep its machinery up-to-date in order to compete, and so need to invest in new technologies on a regular basis.

Legal factors

There is legislation in place to cover, for example, accounting practices, trading practices, employment practices, waste disposal and processing. Existing legislation is not written in stone, and may be amended from time to time. In addition, new legislation is introduced frequently and so every business needs to be aware of the impact of legislation, existing and new, on its business practices.

Environmental/ecological factors

Organizations usually become aware of environmental factors when legislation is enacted, for example, to reduce carbon and sulphur emissions. There are costs associated with the management of such issues, but at the same time a business may wish to emphasize or develop its environmental 'persona' in order to increase its customer-base, where customer expectation is increased in this area.

Activity 9 · 25 mins

S/NVQ C1.1

This Activity may provide the basis of appropriate evidence for your S/NVQ portfolio. If you are intending to take this course of action it might be better to write your answers on separate sheets of paper.

Complete the following chart, noting down those factors that might affect your organization, and you personally and as a manager, over the next three years. You may have to do some research to make sure that your own knowledge is up-to-date. Health and safety officers, personnel or human resource staff, for example, are likely sources of relevant information, in relation to legislative changes.

For example, if your organization needs to invest in new technology to remain competitive, you may be faced with the issue of staff redundancies, a potentially fraught and painful matter. Or, if new environmental legislation is introduced, you may find that your working practices have to change radically to take this into account – indeed, your job may change completely or even disappear.

FACTORS	ORGANISATIONAL IMPACT	PERSONAL IMPACT
POLITICAL		
ECONOMIC		
SOCIAL		
TECHNOLOGICAL		
LEGAL		
ENVIRONMENTAL/ ECOLOGICAL		

Activity 10

5 mins

Reflect upon your findings in Activity 9. Consider each of the factors that you have identified as having an impact upon you as a manager. Now ask yourself this question.

■ Will I be able to deal with these factors using my existing strengths?

Where the answer is 'NO' place an asterisk (*) next to the factor concerned.

4 Confirming your findings

The analyses that you have completed have provided you with a detailed range of information. You should now have a clear sense of your areas of strength and weakness, the areas where you are posed with both opportunities and threats, and where external factors will (or are likely to) affect your future capability.

However, what you have at present is just your own personal assessment. It is important that you confirm your findings by checking them with other people to see whether or not they agree with you.

Activity 11

10 mins

S/NVQ C1.1

This Activity may provide the basis of appropriate evidence for your S/NVQ portfolio. If you are intending to take this course of action it might be better to write your answers on separate sheets of paper.

Complete the left-hand column of the following chart, inserting the relevant detail from your analysis (Activity 8) and the asterisked items from your PESTLE analysis (Activity 9). Leave the commentator's name and job title box blank (the commentator can fill in those details for themselves).

Feedback on personal assessment of current effectiveness

Your name _____   Your job title _____

Commentator's name: _____ Commentator's job title: _____	Findings confirmed? Y/N	Commentator's feedback
My areas of current weakness.		
My potential areas for future development (threats).		
External factors that will require me to develop my existing skills and knowledge.		
This space is for the commentator to add detail on other areas of weakness/development that I should consider.		

Having filled in details of your personal assessment in the left hand column of the chart, photocopy it at least twice. In the next activity you will give a copy to others for their comment and feedback.

4.1 Seeking feedback

Throughout our working lives, and as an integral part of development, we need to seek and receive constructive feedback. Feedback is essential, especially in the early stages of assessing our development needs, because we often see ourselves in a very different way to how others see us. Where we present others with our personal view we can ask them to confirm our own perceptions, and request their suggestions about possible ways forward. This can help to ensure that any development activity you decide to undertake is truly relevant.

To make sure that you get feedback that is constructive you need to do the following.

- Be specific; make it clear **what** you want the feedback on, and say **why** you want it – in this case to support you in becoming more effective.
- Ask for comments on particular areas of weakness. For example, if you say you are weak in asking questions, ask them to either agree or disagree, but ask that they also back this up with an example.
- Set the feedback in context; in this case you are asking for the feedback to help you to find out where you need to think more about personal or professional development.
- Check that you understand what has been offered as feedback. This is easy enough if you ask for verbal feedback, because you can clarify any ambiguities at the time. But where you seek written feedback (using the information from Activity 12 for example), follow this up quickly with a brief discussion. This is important in order to avoid any misunderstanding about what has been written.

For feedback to be valid and useful it should come from a range of different sources. Try and make sure that those offering the feedback are:

- in a position to offer feedback and comment, i.e. someone who works with you/for you or sees you performing your job;
- likely to be honest and constructive, and not just say what they think you might want to hear!

Activity 12

S/NVQ C1.1

This Activity may provide the basis of appropriate evidence for your S/NVQ portfolio. If you are intending to take this course of action it might be better to write your answers on separate sheets of paper.

Give a completed copy of the chart from Activity 11 to at least two people. This might include your line manager, a member of your team and/or a work colleague. Arrange a suitable time with each person separately, to discuss their comments. You should make notes of what they say.

4.2 Completing the picture

Once you have received and checked the feedback from your colleagues about your self-assessment, you will then need to go over it again and summarize the main points of agreement about the areas of weakness that you have identified. This will give you your starting point for the next stage of this workbook – putting your development needs in order of priority, and specifying how you could go about meeting them.

Activity 13

Using the material you have gathered when discussing your self-assessment with your colleagues, write down a complete list of all the areas you have identified and agreed as needing some developmental input. Don't worry about priorities at this point, we'll look at that later in the next session.

_____

_____

_____

_____

_____

_____

Self-assessment 1

10 mins

For questions 1 to 4 complete the sentences with a suitable word or words from the following list.

STORAGE   KNOWLEDGE   PEOPLE   SHOULD
SOURCES   TASKS   SKILLS   WEAKNESSES
STRENGTHS   MUST

1   Job-related information comes in a range of forms and from a variety of
    _____

2   Every job is made up of key _____ and activities

3   In order to be effective we need a combination of skills, _____
    and personal attributes.

4   Weaknesses that _____ be addressed quickly are those that will
    involve job requirements that are fundamental to the overall day-to-day
    performance of your job.

5   What are the factors that comprise a PESTLE analysis?

    _____

    _____

    _____

    _____

    _____

    _____

6   Why is seeking feedback essential?

    _____

    _____

7   How can we make sure that feedback is valid and reliable?

    _____

    _____

    _____

Answers to these questions can be found on pages 77–78.

5 Summary

■ To become more effective we all need a starting point. We need to know what our present job requires of us and where we might be falling short. Even top managers need to reassess their performance once in a while, so this is a normal part of the development process.

■ Every job is made up of key tasks and activities, and in order to complete these key tasks and activities, the jobholder should:

  ■ possess skills relevant to the tasks and activities;
  ■ hold knowledge that underpins, or supports these skills;
  ■ be able to behave appropriately within the environment of the job.

■ Overall the role of a manager is likely to include managing:

  ■ activities and quality;
  ■ other people, yourself and relationships;
  ■ financial and physical resources;
  ■ communication and information.

■ Throughout our working lives, and as an integral part of development, we need to seek and receive constructive feedback. Feedback is essential, particularly at the early stages of self-assessment, because we often see ourselves in a very different way to how others see us.

Session B
Choosing development activities that suit your needs

1 Introduction

Having completed the activities in Session A, you should by now have a clear picture of the personal and professional developmental issues you face as a manager. Depending on what you have come up with, it's possible that you may feel a bit disheartened. If, for example, there are several issues that you realize need addressing urgently, or perhaps just one that seems to loom rather large and urgent. This is a natural reaction we all experience when we're facing up to those areas where we fall short of our ideal! How can I convert those weaknesses into strengths? How will I cope with that threat? However, it may also have encouraged you to be reminded of exactly how much you do know, and where your strengths and expertise lie. You may also have been pleasantly surprised by some of your colleagues' comments.

This session begins by looking at what 'development' means, and how it differs from two similar terms – training and learning. The session then builds on the work you did in Session A. First we will look at a simple procedure for enabling you to put your various development needs into a logical order. Then we look at how you can begin to convert your weaknesses into strengths by the process of setting yourself workable **performance objectives**.

The main part of the session looks at the relationship between the various development activities available to you, and your own process of learning, known as your **preferred learning style**. By having a clear understanding of the relationship between them, you will be better able to find a focus in the quite complex area of personal and professional development activity.

When looking at possible **forms of development activity**, you need to take two things into account before making your decision. There's the type of activity itself (we describe the most important of these first), and then there's the question of which of these are actually available to you in practice.

Every individual is different and no single development activity will suit everyone. However, most of us benefit from taking different approaches to learning, and it's crucial not to dismiss activities that don't seem to suit you at first glance, because by doing so you may miss useful opportunities.

By the end of this session, you should have a clear picture of which forms of development activity are available to you. You should also have a better idea of how your own learning process either fits with those activities, or where it might be at odds with them and how you might deal with this.

You'll then be equipped to move on to Session C, where you look at the practicalities of preparing a personal development plan.

2 What is 'development'?

There are whole books on the subject of development, and it's not the aim of this workbook to bog you down in the discussion of definitions! Having said that, a definition of some sort is necessary. So far, we've been using the term 'development' without really making it clear what we mean by it.

There is a tendency to confuse 'development' with 'training' and 'learning'. In fact, they refer to different things, and it's important to be clear about the differences. We'll briefly discuss training and learning first, in order to get a more precise idea of what 'development' means.

Training

Training is perhaps the most straightforward term. Training is a planned series of activities that enable the trainees to do something they couldn't do before. An expert demonstrates how to do something, and provides guidance to the trainees. For example, a gardener can be trained to use a chain-saw, a receptionist can be trained to use a switchboard or a graphic designer to use QuarkXpress. Training is usually linked to limited objectives, where we will be able to do something, or will know something, that we could not do or did not know before we were trained. The success of a training programme will depend mainly on how well it is organized and on the skill of the trainer.

Learning

Learning is perhaps most usefully defined as absorbing new information in such a way that we can apply it in practice. We learn in all sorts of different ways in the course of our lives – we learn how to talk and walk, we learn how to cook or write an essay, we learn how to play football and get on with other people. These examples involve very different processes, but all of them depend partly on our individual capabilities. Some people become master chefs, others can't even learn to boil an egg. Some people become award-winning writers, others avoid putting pen to paper again once they leave school. Learning therefore depends largely on our individual aptitude.

In summary then, we might describe the difference between training and learning as follows.

- Training is the input of information from outside.
- Learning is the internal process of absorbing and understanding that information so that we can put it into practice.

If you want to know more about training and learning, you can study *Delivering Training* in this series.

Training and learning are both aspects of **development**.

Activity 14 · 2 mins

Write down your own brief definition of the word 'development'.

_____

_____

When we ask different people what they understand by this word we get a range of responses, including:

- "... getting better at my job";
- "... changing what we do for the better";
- "... making the most of what I can already do";
- "... taking different approaches to the way I do things";
- "... going beyond what I can do now".

Your definition may be different, but it probably contained a strong sense of movement and change.

Development

We can think of development as adding to something that is already there – a process of growth, of building on an existing foundation. Development is about personal and professional evolution and advancement; becoming better equipped to deal with the changes that affect us now and in the future. While development involves both training and learning it is more than the two of them put together. It also involves other, more personal factors, which are not easily defined.

Donna and Blondel were good friends who hadn't seen one another for many years. Donna had got married and had a family, while Blondel had developed a successful career in accountancy.

'I really haven't done anything much', said Donna with some embarrassment, 'Just been a very traditional housewife looking after the kids and hubby! You seem to have done lots of interesting things, Blondel. Networking with all those high-powered people! And that corporate merger you were involved in sounded really fascinating, and you seem to be so confident and knowledgeable. I must seem very dull in comparison.'

'Actually, you don't!' said Blondel, 'The way you described dealing with Jenny's learning difficulties and how you managed everything when Bill had that car accident make me realise how little I'm able to deal with everyday life. I'm red hot with the paperwork and I love the buzz of corporate networking, but if my Mum became seriously ill, I don't know how I'd cope!'

Activity 15 · 5 mins

Jot down a few brief notes about how these two very different people could be said to have developed.

_____

_____

_____

_____

You may have noted the following things.

■ Blondel has developed a much greater self-confidence in the business world than she has in everyday life.
■ Donna has developed personal qualities such as endurance and the ability to care for people over a long period of time.
■ Blondel has developed her ambition and networking abilities.
■ Donna has developed her maternal qualities, but feels she's lacking in the ability to deal with more objective matters in the outside world.

Donna probably won't have had any training for the life she's chosen, but has developed considerably as a person nonetheless. Blondel will have been highly trained (and had the aptitude for) accountancy in order to get where she is now. However, although she's developed professionally, she seems to feel less confident of her abilities at a day-to-day human level.

You have probably already thought about the fact that completing this workbook is itself a professional development activity.

Activity 16

5 mins

Think about this workbook, *Becoming More Effective*. Take a few minutes now to look through it, noting the various features it contains.

■ How does this workbook become part of your training? What features of the workbook meet the definition of training we gave earlier in this section?

_____

_____

■ How will you be able to demonstrate the learning that you may acquire from completion of this workbook?

_____

_____

■ Briefly summarize how you think that completion of this workbook will contribute to your development.

_____

_____

There are no correct answers to this activity, since they will depend on the nature of your job, but we can give general indications.

- The workbook has clear objectives, as set out on page vii, and can therefore be seen as a form of training. In addition, it has been produced by people who are expert in the field of development.
- You will be able to demonstrate any learning acquired from this workbook by applying it to your role as a manager.
- Completing the workbook will enable you to grow and advance in your ability to do your job, and perhaps consider new career moves.

3 Your development needs – in order of priority

You have examined the skills, knowledge and personal attribute requirements needed in your current job, analysed your areas of strength and weakness and sought feedback on your findings. The next stage is to begin prioritising your actual development needs: in what order do you need to tackle them?

A simple approach is to ask yourself the following questions.

- Are there any weaknesses that MUST be addressed quickly? These will be those that affect your day-to-day performance of your job.
- Which weaknesses SHOULD be addressed over the next 3–6 months? (i.e. where you're only involved in the activity on an irregular basis, for example appraisal interviews.)
- Which weaknesses COULD be addressed on a longer-term basis? For example, weaknesses that are less concerned with your current job than with your career aspirations.

Activity 17 · 10 mins

Look at your list of identified and agreed weaknesses, which you drew up at the end of Session A. Put these weaknesses in order of priority, using the three questions above. Those weaknesses that MUST be addressed urgently should be labelled as 1, those that SHOULD be addressed within the medium term as 2, and finally those that COULD be addressed in the long term as 3.

Of course, if you have only identified one development need, the choice is simple, but you still need to be clear about what sort of need it is, and which of these three priorities it is.

_____

_____

_____

_____

_____

_____

Next to each development need you have listed here, note whether it is a skill, knowledge or a personal attribute that you need to acquire or develop.

This activity should have given you a sharper focus on your immediate development needs. We now move on to see how they can be turned into strengths by creating practical performance objectives.

4 Specifying your objectives

To change a weakness into a strength, you need to set yourself precise objectives that will work in practice. These can be used to measure your performance, so that you can tell when the weakness has become a strength.

For example, you may have identified an area of weakness such as 'I'm not up-to-date with the legislation about X.' Your objective might then be stated as 'To become familiar with the new legislation about X, and be able to explain it to the members of my team.'

Let's look at how we do this in a bit more detail.

Activity 18

Maddi manages a team of eight researchers in a company that carries out market research by telephone and records the details on a database, for different companies across the UK. The team usually works in smaller groups for particular clients. The research projects change regularly, so Maddi has to brief her team on a weekly basis, allocating clients to the various smaller groups.

She has found out that she does not do this very effectively. Her team does not absorb the information that she gives them. Sometimes the team members are not sure who their clients for the week are, and this results in confusion. Essential tasks are not carried out by the right people, or are not carried out at all.

After several complaints, Maddi has realised that her weakness lies in how she gives out information, which does not enable her staff to carry out their work in a way that meets customer requirements. She has also realised that this weakness is a priority that must be addressed, because it is a task that she carries out on a weekly basis.

What does Maddi need to do that she is not doing now?

_____

_____

_____

One of the things you may have stated is that, during the weekly briefings, Maddi needs to give out information to all members of the team in a way that enables them to do their job, on a week-by-week basis.

What we have done is produce a 'statement of need', also called a **performance objective**. The performance objective changes a weakness into a positive statement of something that needs to be done. In other words, once Maddi is able to perform as stated, the weakness will have been addressed.

But we still don't know how this will be done. The objective is couched in very general terms. How do we bring it down to a practical level? Let's look at the different qualities a performance objective needs to have if it is to be of any immediate value.

In summary, objectives need to SMART. This means that an objective should be:

- **S**pecific
- **M**easurable
- **A**chievable
- **R**elevant
- **T**ime bound.

Specific

Specific means that the objective should state what actions need to be carried out, using language that is easily understood by everyone concerned. *'Conduct weekly briefings, giving out information to all members of the team'* is a specific statement of Maddi's task.

Measurable

For an objective to be **measurable** it needs to be set in a way that it can be assessed. If there is no measurement attached to the objective, such as '... *in a way that enables them to do their job, on a week-by-week basis'*, it will be difficult to decide when it has been achieved, whether there has been a shortfall or where requirements have been exceeded. If each member of the team cannot explain what is required of him or her at the end of each briefing, and if the work is not carried out as stated, then Maddi has not achieved her performance objective.

Achievable

If an objective is to be **achievable**, it must take into account the resources available – including the resource of time. Maddi needs to set aside a particular amount of time per week for this briefing and allow herself sufficient preparation time – this might mean producing short briefings beforehand, in writing, for the different groups. To ensure that this objective is achievable, Maddi may need to review how her time is allocated across the rest of the week. The objective also needs to take into account the capabilities of the individual. For example, if Maddi's problem is not lack of time, but the skill needed to write a clear brief, she may need extra help with this.

Relevant

For an objective to be **relevant** it needs to make sense to the individual in terms of their job role, and to support the overall objectives of the department and the business. Maddi's overall responsibility is for the performance of her team, and these briefings are an essential part of this responsibility – hence this objective is clearly relevant to Maddi.

Time bound

Finally objectives need to be **time bound**. Questions to consider include the following.

- When must the objective be achieved by?
- When will the objective be reviewed?

Given that it is a regular part of her job, Maddi's objective is a high priority, so the objective needs to be achieved within the next month or two, at the very most.

Reviewing objectives is essential, in order to monitor your progress. If the objective needs to be achieved in, say, three months time, then the reviews should be carried out at least once a month. The person who carries out this review is likely to be the person with whom the objective was agreed, for example your line manager.

In the next session we will discuss how to review your performance objectives.

Activity 19 · 10 mins

Return to Activity 17 and take **two** of the areas of weakness that you have listed as priority 1.

_____

_____

Now convert these weaknesses into SMART performance objectives, i.e. **state what you will be able to do** when you have addressed these weaknesses, and they have been converted into strengths. As you do this, look back at the list of qualities that a SMART objective needs to have, to remind yourself of what each of those qualities involves.

_____

_____

_____

_____

_____

_____

Once you have undertaken a relevant development activity, you should be able to fulfil the performance objective.

5 Forms of development activity

Development activities take a variety of forms. Because personal and professional development is a different experience for each of us, it is important to recognize that there is such a variety of possibilities.

Activity 20 · 2 mins

List all the different types, or forms, of development activity that you can think of.

_____

_____

_____

_____

_____

You may have listed some or all of the following.

- Training courses and programmes.
- Coaching.
- Mentoring.
- Distance learning – using workbooks, possibly with tutor support, or through computer-based learning programmes accessible on-line.
- Work-based projects.
- Computer-based training, possibly using CD-ROM material.
- Planned or guided reading.

We will now look at these forms of development and explore what is involved in each. One important clue to the type of activity you might consider as you read the descriptions that follow, is whether it's likely to be something you will enjoy. Your enjoyment of it will depend upon your preferred learning style, which we've mentioned before and will come back to later in this session.

5.1 Training courses and programmes

As we said earlier, these usually involve learning new skills, knowledge or ways of working. Training courses and programmes should have clearly stated objectives or learning outcomes, so that the participants know what to expect and can gauge the effectiveness of the training once it's completed. Look at the objectives before you start a training course, because this will help you and your line manager focus on what the training provides before you actually attend.

Training courses will be delivered through a variety of approaches. These approaches are designed to suit the learning styles of the different participants and keep the trainees interested, so a training programme will involve more than one training method. For example, demonstrations, presentations and discussions may all be used.

Advantages of training courses and programmes are:

- there is an exchange of ideas between the participants;
- teaching by experts in the subject;
- focus on particular skills, knowledge or personal attributes;
- the needs of a number of people are met in a cost effective way.

Disadvantages might include that:

- the costs can be high in some cases;
- the content may not be equally relevant to all participants;
- attendance may require time away from work.

5.2 Coaching

This is a one-to-one activity. Coaching is a process where an individual is actively supported in solving a problem or performing a task more effectively. It may also be used when a manager needs to delegate some part of his or her job to a member of the team. However, a coach will be anyone who is in possession of the expertise and skills that are to be handed on to the less experienced person. For example, the first line manager may coach a team member in how to allocate tasks to other members of the workforce, or how to write reports. Or one team member may need to coach another in an aspect of their job when work processes or procedures change.

Coaching can provide excellent opportunities for development within the workplace, using existing resources and expertise.

Advantages of coaching are:

- the team or department has more than one person who can fill a particular role or function if necessary;
- the person being coached does not have to leave work in order to develop their skills;
- the skills and experience are immediately relevant to the job;
- it makes the job more interesting;
- both people involved are working with someone they know;
- it is a very cost effective form of development.

Disadvantages are that:

- it can be very time consuming;
- singling out one individual in this way may cause resentment among other members of the workforce;
- the person who receives coaching may be encouraged to challenge the coach's authority;
- the coach may pass on poor working habits or practices;
- the coach may not be very good in this role, even if they are good at their job.

5.3 Mentoring

The mentor is an experienced person who helps the individual they are mentoring to clarify their professional goals. The mentor can discuss with the mentee what they want to achieve and how they can best go about attaining this (e.g. by acquiring certain skills and/or experience). They then act as a means of support and guidance as the mentee goes about achieving their goals over a period of time. At the end of the mentoring process the mentor and mentee review the process and review the goals if necessary.

A mentor is likely to be someone with experience of an organisation, a job, or a particular way of working. In many cases, a mentor can help an individual to access resources (such as information or professional contacts) that were previously unknown to them or out of their reach. Usually, the mentor is not someone in authority with whom the individual works directly (such as their line manager), since mentoring is more like an informal partnership than an authority relationship.

The advantages and disadvantages are similar to those of coaching, although because the mentoring relationship does not overlap with work roles, the person being mentored is not singled out from their colleagues in the same way.

5.4 Distance learning

Distance learning enables individuals to undertake development opportunities and approaches to learning in their own time and at their own pace, and without having to attend formal courses. It's also called 'flexible' or 'open' learning. Distance learning can include:

- written open learning workbooks and packs, like this one;
- audio visual learning – through tapes, CDs, television programmes, videos, DVDs;
- computer-based training, by way of CD-ROM training packages, on-line training or on-line conferencing.

For distance learning to be effective it is important that individuals are given adequate support. This might mean that individuals on distance/flexible learning programmes have regular access to a tutor, or to fellow learners at workshops. Programmes of distance learning can be cost-effective, and flexible as they can be adapted to suit individual needs and circumstances.

Its **advantages** are that is is flexible, the learner progresses at the pace most suitable to him or her, and it is usually less expensive than an attendance course. **Disadvantages** include the fact that students may work almost entirely alone, which can make motivation difficult.

Activity 21

Write down what you personally have found to be the advantages and disadvantages of learning by this method when using this workbook.

_____

_____

_____

5.5 Work-based projects

Designing work-based projects linked to your performance objectives is a worthwhile and practical approach. Such projects can be cost-effective and cost-efficient, because they will make use of existing resources, and may in fact be designed to maximize the use of these resources. Development becomes part and parcel of work, as individuals will be expected to stretch themselves, applying their skills and knowledge in new ways. Work-based projects can also help with transferability of skills and knowledge, especially where they meet both the needs of the learner and those of the organization.

Helena had recently begun working as the first line manager for the office administration team. The team was based in the administration block of a large university, and was responsible for processing accommodation requests for new students, as well as post-graduate students. When she started the job, Helena's line manager talked through the current situation and highlighted the fact that recent computerization of the system had caused a number of problems. Paperwork was duplicated, particularly where members of the team were still operating the old system, keying in data only to satisfy the needs of the IT department – this had resulted in three different sets of accommodation records being available for one student.

Helena and her manager had agreed that – as part of her development, and in order to be able to assure the quality of the records (a key part of her job) – she would carry out a thorough analysis of the current situation. She would hold individual discussions with all team members and draw up a recommended plan of action, including suggestions for training and development. She would hold a one hour weekly meeting with her line manager to review progress, and check that she was working along the right lines.

This example summarizes an approach to work-based projects that is practical and relevant to the individual's performance at work. Helena is developing her skills, knowledge and personal attributes while solving a problem in a real work situation, which is both cost and time efficient and effective.

It can be tempting to see work-based projects as being always the best way to develop at work, because they focus on the work at hand. However, such projects must be carefully thought out. They must be linked closely to the learner's performance objective(s) as well as to organizational needs, so that the learner feels that the experience was useful and relevant. Where you wish to use this form of development, you need to be sure that you will receive solid support and guidance. It may be most effectively used along with coaching or mentoring (see above).

5.6 Computer-based training (CBT)

As we become more information-technology literate, computer-based training is becoming more widespread. It can take the form of CD-ROM material that takes the learner through different scenarios, asking you to make choices, or where you interact with the package and learn through the decisions that you take. These programs may include text, images, and also audio or video material.

This form of development depends upon the computer resources available. Such programs may also be available through the Internet. It is likely that in the future, 'online' and 'distance' learning will come to mean the same thing.

The **advantages** of CBT are:

- development can usually be done in modular form, so the learner can pick and choose what they need from a range of modules;
- the learners go at their own pace, and can repeat their studies as often as they like until they feel proficient;
- it is relatively cheap.

Its **disadvantages** are that:

- the isolation does not suit some people;
- not everyone is happy working with a machine;
- it is not always suitable if the topic you want to study is developing rapidly, since the material will date quickly.

5.7 Planned or guided reading

Planned or guided reading is a form of development that enables you to expand your knowledge in a particular field or area. Sources will include:

- the Internet;
- professional journals and publications;
- books;
- specialist sections of newspapers.

As mentioned above, the Internet is a vast source of information about every imaginable subject. Because the array of sources is so wide (and of varying quality), your reading needs to be planned or guided by someone who knows the field. You will need to focus on the area of knowledge that will enable you to fulfil your agreed performance objective.

One obvious source of access to books and journals is your local library. Even if its own stock is quite limited, it can supply you with books or journals from other libraries, using centralized ordering systems. You may come across a journal that contains regular and relevant information, either in relation to your current role or to your future career plans. Many journals are available on-line; however, you may have to pay a subscription fee to gain access to some of them.

Research skills are very important if planned or guided reading is to be your choice of development activity. It is essential to be able to know what information is available and from where, and know how to draw out the key features of what you read. A disadvantage can be that it is an activity that the learner does alone, and this can make motivation difficult.

Activity 22 · 3 mins

Make a brief note of those activities that attracted you, and those you wanted to dismiss as possibilities.

_____

_____

_____

_____

_____

_____

We'll look at the issues raised by your answers to this activity later in this session.

5.8 Access to development activities

The development activities open to you will depend upon the following.

- Resources available at work – for example a comprehensive training programme may be available, or there could be the facility for using personal computer facilities for working with CD-ROM training packages.
- Skilled personnel – for example, where experienced individuals are able to coach or mentor individuals.
- Availability of time and/or financial support – some individuals choose to use their own time at home, or companies sometimes offer individuals financial support to pursue their studies outside work.

Of course, these are not the only reasons why you may, or may not, take up any of the various development activities. But it is important that you know which ones are available and accessible to you, because your development plan (which you will be developing in the next session of this workbook) needs to be valid and reliable. It should not be a wish list of development opportunities, but needs to reflect reality.

5.9 Keeping your objectives in mind

Whatever activities you choose, you need to keep your performance objectives in mind. Constant reference to, and periodic revision of, your development plan will help you to focus on development activities that remain relevant to your particular needs.

6 Ways of learning

Having looked at what's on offer in the world outside, we'll now look at how you yourself like to learn.

The next activity is designed to help you begin to explore your own preferred learning style.

Activity 23

5 mins

Briefly describe any development activity that you have been involved in recently. (For example, was it a training course, or did someone coach you in a particular feature of your job?)

_____

_____

_____

What did the development activity enable you to do and/or know, that you did not do and/or know beforehand?

_____

_____

Summarize briefly what you learned as a result of the activity.

_____

_____

What features of the development activity helped you to learn? (For example, the way the course leader structured the event, using exercises and discussion, or the detailed handouts provided.)

_____

_____

_____

Was there anything you particularly enjoyed, or disliked, about the experience?

_____

_____

Your response to this activity will begin to give you some idea of how you like (or don't like) to learn. What you found helpful and enjoyed about the experience will give you an indication of your preferred way of learning.

For example, the information may have been delivered in a way that you found easy to take in. Or you might have got most out of the information that you were given by using it actively in an exercise. Perhaps you found that, being given the time to reflect on what you had been told enabled you to absorb it more fully. You may have felt stimulated to learn by being with other people, or perhaps you found them a distraction. You may have mentioned more than one reason in your answer.

The development activity you considered in this activity will probably have included one or more of the three main ways of learning:

- imitation;
- instruction;
- experience.

We all use one or other of these ways of learning at different points in life and for different reasons.

As children, we often **imitate** other children or adults we admire and want to resemble; in adult life we might imitate someone whom we feel is a good role model for some form of behaviour ('Now how would So-and-so behave in this situation?'). Or we might imitate how an expert carries out an action ('I see, he holds the mattock with both hands, with one half way down the shaft, and doesn't raise it above his shoulder. Now let me see if I can do that. How does it feel when I do it right?')

We're all familiar with **instruction** as a form of learning from our experience of being taught various subjects at school. In fact, for many people, instruction is learning, and if they've had unsatisfying experiences at school, they're likely to avoid it later if at all possible. However, in adult life, instruction remains an important part of some development activities, such as training courses.

'Experience is the name that everyone gives to their mistakes ... Life would be very dull without them.' (Oscar Wilde.)

Experience is in some ways a more complex form of learning than the other two, although we learn from experience all through our lives – or don't! This quip highlights the truth that experience alone doesn't necessarily teach us anything. Learning from experience only occurs when you actively think and have feelings about the experience and learn the lessons it provides. A good way of thinking about this process is given in the figure below.

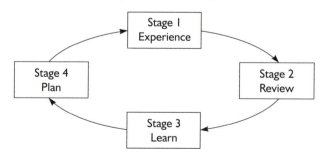

The experiential learning cycle

As the name suggests, in stage 1 of the cycle we start with an experience of some kind. Let's take the simple example of waiting for a bus, where we wait for a long time. The second stage involves the learner in reviewing the experience, unravelling the positive and negative features of the experience at stage 1. For example, there was no bus shelter, and it was raining, however, we had an interesting conversation with someone else at the bus stop. At stage 2 we would need to consider what happened, why it happened and the consequences of the experience overall. In this case, we were late for an appointment, we got very wet and spent a few days in bed with a cold, but the long wait also meant that we made a new friend. At stage 3 we identify what we can learn from what happened, by possibly stating:

- 'I should have taken an umbrella . . .';
- 'I didn't anticipate the problem of being late . . .';
- 'Perhaps I could have taken the tube . . .';
- 'I enjoy unexpected meetings with new people . . .'.

At the fourth stage we plan what we will do next time (e.g. take an umbrella, allow extra time, be more open to the possibilities at bus stops), building on what we have learned from our journey through the experiential learning cycle.

Experiential learning is probably the most effective form of learning, because it involves using all our capabilities in an active way, rather than just accepting what others tell us in a passive way.

6.1 Learning styles

Most of us do not travel equally comfortably through the different phases of the experiential learning cycle. For a number of reasons, we often stay lodged at one or another stage. Some of us are happy to involve ourselves in different experiences, without ever moving forward to review what happened, or to learn from that experience. We enjoy the activity for the sake of the activity, but find it less easy to learn from the experience. Many of us enjoy the process of making plans, but often don't get to the point of putting them into practice.

EXTENSIONS 1 AND 2 You may like to follow up the subject of learning styles by looking at the books by Honey and Mumford listed at the end of this workbook.

Each stage of the experiential learning cycle we looked at above is connected with a particular style of learning. The various ways in which people learn were divided by Honey and Mumford into four basic styles.

- Activist (Stage 1).
- Reflector (Stage 2).
- Theorist (Stage 3).
- Pragmatist (Stage 4).

Spend a few minutes studying the chart below, and think about which most closely resembles your own preferred learning style. (You may have more than one.)

Learning style and brief description
Activist ■ Gets fully involved in new experiences. ■ Enthusiastic about new experiences. ■ Tends to act first, considers the consequences later. ■ Thrives on challenge.
Reflector ■ Likes to stand back and think about what they have experienced. ■ Tends to put off reaching final conclusion as long as possible. ■ Gathers lots of information from lots of different sources – uses this to come to a conclusion. ■ Tends to be thoughtful, considers all angles and implications. ■ Prefers to take a back seat in group situations. ■ Likes to observe others, rather than being involved.
Theorist ■ Takes a logical step-by-step approach to problem-solving. ■ Builds facts and establishes theories. ■ Tends to like perfection. ■ Analyses, using principles, models, theories and systems.
Pragmatist ■ Keen to try out new ideas, theories and approaches to see if they work in practice. ■ Experiments with new ideas. ■ Wants to try out new ideas from courses. ■ Acts quickly, confidently where ideas are interesting. ■ Impatient with extended analysis and open-ended discussion. ■ Takes practical approach to problem-solving.

Gordon became Customer Service Manager last year. He has attended many different training courses, covering everything from finance to handling conflict. Recently his manager came to him to ask him for a brief evaluation of the courses he had attended.

Gordon realized that he had found the least useful courses to be those that had involved a lot of role-playing and group exercises – he generally left the event feeling that he had wasted his time. He had also attended lectures at the local college and found that where one person was giving out information, supported by handouts and his own notes, he gained a lot of information that he could think about later.

In the course of his evaluation, Gordon noted that: 'I like thinking about the theories and ideas of others, working out where they might work in my department'.

Activity 24

2 mins

Which learning style (or styles) does Gordon prefer?

While it is important to recognize your preferred learning style, it is also important not to box yourself into a corner in doing so. The way we learn most easily naturally influences the forms of development that we choose, and we might ignore ways of learning that are different.

It is also valuable to know your preferred style when it comes to evaluating the effectiveness of any development activity. If you feel that it was not as successful as you had hoped, it could have been because the approach may not have suited your preferred learning style, rather than because there was anything wrong with the activity itself. Gordon is most probably a combination of Reflector and Theorist, but this means that he has tended to dismiss an approach that doesn't fit with these styles of learning.

If you develop a variety of learning styles, you will be able to take advantage of a wider range of development opportunities. Of course, we do not always have the luxury of choice when selecting forms of development to meet our needs. We may have to accept that the opportunity available does not really suit our preferred learning style. However, we can use this self-knowledge to get the most out of what's actually on offer.

Activity 25

20 mins

At this point, you might like to begin to check your personal preferences against what is realistic in practice. For example, if you have realized that you need to become more skilled in dealing with conflict in your team, and also that you enjoy a group learning situation, find out if there are workshops available, either locally or through your workplace. If, for whatever reason, this is not realistic, you may need to consider settling for another distance learning workbook on the topic.

The first two sessions of this workbook have helped you to work out what your development needs and performance objectives are, and have examined the range of development opportunities and how these relate to your preferred learning style. With this information, you can now begin to prepare your own personal development plan, and we'll do this in the final session.

Self-assessment 2

10 mins

1 Briefly describe the difference between training, learning and development.

_____

_____

_____

_____

_____

_____

2 In order to change a weakness into a strength, you need to set yourself clear

_____ _____.

3 In order to be effective, you need to be able to set yourself performance objectives that are:

- S _____
- M _____
- A _____
- R _____
- T _____.

4 Fill in the missing words in the following diagram

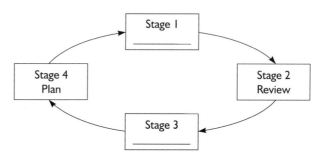

5 List four types of development activity.

_____

_____

_____

_____

6 You will find a development activity either attractive or unattractive, depending on your _____ _____ _____ .

7 What are the four basic learning styles?

_____

_____

_____

_____

You will find the answers to these questions on page 78.

7 Summary

■ The terms 'development', 'training, and 'learning' are used interchangeably, but they do not mean the same things. Training and learning are aspects of development.

■ Development is about personal growth and advancement. Training is concerned with learning particular, limited skills. Learning is concerned with understanding and being able to apply the new knowledge in your working life.

■ When tackling your training and development needs, you need to divide them into immediate, medium-term and longer-term needs.

■ For objectives to be effective, and to reflect your understanding of what you need to be able to do, they need to be SMART: Specific, Measurable, Achievable, Relevant and Time bound.

■ A performance objective states what you will be able to do once you have converted a weakness into a strength. It specifies a development need. Once you have completed a relevant development activity, you will be able to fulfil the performance objective.

■ Different forms of development activity will be appropriate for different individuals. No one approach will suit everyone. However, it is important not to rule out forms of development that don't fit with your preferred learning style, otherwise you may miss out on opportunities. The activities that are actually available may not suit your learning style.

■ The forms of development activity most commonly available are: training courses and programmes, coaching, mentoring, distance learning, work-based projects, computer- based training, planned or guided reading.

■ When deciding on which activities are available to you, you will need to take into account:

  ■ the resources available at work;
  ■ whether there are people who are skilled enough to provide coaching or mentoring;
  ■ the availability of time and/or financial support.

■ The four learning styles are: activist, reflector, theorist and pragmatist.

Session C
Making it happen

1 Introduction

In the last session you began to look at the different forms of development that might be possible for you, and to examine your own personal learning style. In this session we will construct a personal development plan.

To become more effective, you need to take responsibility not only for producing a development plan for yourself, but also for taking steps to make sure the plan is put into effect.

Once you have turned your plans into reality, you will need to assess their effect. You'll need to ask questions about the value of what you've done, what you now do differently and better, and what you would do differently next time. In order to ask these questions you will need to log, review and examine your development activities in a critical way.

Working through this session will enable you to construct your own personal development plan (PDP), and look at how to put it into practice. It also discusses why it is necessary to review and evaluate your PDP from time to time, and how you can do this.

2 The Personal Development Plan (PDP)

A personal development plan is the result of a process of agreement and discussion. Your manager will probably need to approve the content of your personal development plan, particularly if he or she is responsible for allocating resources for personal and professional development. Your plan may need to be in line with the needs of the department and the organisation as well as meeting your own objectives.

We have supplied below a format for a PDP that you can either adopt as it stands or adapt for your own purposes. The plan used as an illustration here has been developed around the example of Maddi's development need (see page 32 of Session B), but it is not the only way her performance objective could be met. As you can see, a mix of development forms has been used, with an emphasis on existing resources.

Take a few minutes to look at Maddi's development plan. Obviously it only contains one defined need and objective. For your own PDP, you may need to provide more space to allow for further needs and objectives, or that you want to have different headings.

PERSONAL DEVELOPMENT PLAN

Example

Name: Maddi Edgerns

Job Role: Market Research Phone Team Manager

Line Manager: Arnold Martins

Start Date: 24 April 2002

Development need & performance objective	Achievement of performance objective by	Form(s) of development & resources required/date if available	Method of evaluation for each form of development	Review dates	Comments etc.
Need to give information more clearly so staff can do their jobs.		Team briefing 1 day course (£50 & cover for team supervision) 24 May 02	Brief managers on key learning points from course – 30.5.02	3.6.02	
Conduct weekly briefings, giving out information to all members of the team in a way that enables them to do their job, on a week-by-week basis.	1.7.02	Identify and read up on briefing skills and approaches; copy of 'Presentation Skills for Managers' and handbook produced by marketing team	Production of list of key points to add to those from course – 3.6.02	2.6.02	
		Observe Arnold and two other managers briefing their teams – before 24.5.02 (time away from printshop; excused from writing monthly report)	Discussion on key points raised from observation – 30.5.02	24.6.02	
		Be observed and get feedback from Arnold for two team briefings – 6.6.02 & 20.6.02 (time to review after the event)	Hold discussions with 3 team members who attended the briefing, check they know what they are now supposed to do – review if work carried out as set out at briefing		

Activity 26

2 mins

Why is it important to include the kind of detail evident in Maddi's development plan?

What problems could arise if not enough detail is included ?

_____

_____

_____

A fully detailed plan will help everyone – yourself and your line manager, and any other relevant people such as your company training manager – to build a clear picture of the **aim** of the development activities. At the same time, it will be immediately obvious what **forms** development will take, as well as indicating what **resources** are needed. The plan can be used as a discussion document when negotiating resources for development.

If a personal development plan does not contain the necessary detail it is all too easy to forget what was intended in the first place. A formal, detailed, agreed personal development plan can provide a practical and valuable source of information and review within the workplace.

Problems that can arise from a personal development plan without enough detail might include:

■ restricted access to the necessary resources;
■ no time for the development activity itself, or for a proper evaluation of it.

Your completed personal development plan should show the **order of priority** of each need and its related **performance objective**. The dates for high priority needs are likely to be fast approaching, and there may also be dates for those that are less urgent. Including definite dates is a good idea, because they will help to focus your mind when you come to review the plan. When drawing up deadlines, it's best to avoid terms like 'ongoing', which are vague, and likely to mean that nothing is ever done about that particular issue.

A personal development plan needs to be seen and treated as a practical working document that is used in discussions (for example, at appraisal and performance review) and which also acts as an organizing reference point – it is an essential document in a manager's working life.

PERSONAL DEVELOPMENT PLAN

Name:
Job Role:
Line Manager:

Start Date:

Development need & performance objective	Achievement of performance objective by	Form(s) of development & resources required/date if available	Method of evaluation for each form of development	Review dates	Comments etc.

Activity 27

20 mins

Portfolio of evidence

S/NVQ C1.1

This Activity may provide the basis of appropriate evidence for your S/NVQ portfolio. If you are intending to take this course of action it might be better to write your answers on separate sheets of paper.

Using the PDP form given here (revised if necessary), begin to create a rough draft outline of your own PDP. Depending on your preference, you might want to use either pencil on hard copy (if so, it's useful to make several blank copies), or key it in on screen. Use the list of development needs and performance objectives you have identified in the course of this workbook.

You won't be able to complete the whole form just yet, only the first two columns. As you can see, there are parts of it, in particular methods of evaluation, which we haven't covered yet. As you work through the rest of this session, you will continue to build up your PDP as you go along.

3 From planning to action

Moving from a development plan to a practical development activity is not always quite as straightforward as it might seem. Certainly a plan is the ideal starting point – you have details of what you need to achieve, in the form of one or more objectives. You will also have a list of development activities that you will undertake and resources you will need in order to fulfil the objective(s). Dates for review will also be in place. So what happens next? Well, that's partly up to you!

Your own attitude to the development activity itself is an important factor and will affect its success to some extent. Our personal development is our own responsibility, and it is essential that we take a positive attitude towards it – positive involvement is more likely to result in a positive outcome.

Activity 28 · 5 mins

Reluctantly, Glyn has agreed with the training department that he needs to develop his presentation skills. He is asked more frequently than before to give presentations both to staff and to clients, and it is an area where he tends to 'fly by the seat of his pants'. The training department has arranged for him to attend a one-day presentation skills course at a local college. The other trainees on the course are from other companies.

Glyn is very busy at work and resents the amount of time that he has to spend away from the office. In addition, one of the other team members made a sarcastic remark about him 'having a day off', which annoyed him. He arrives at the training event in an irritable mood, very aware of the work that will pile up in his absence, and still annoyed at his colleague's sarcasm.

His irritation and resentment mean that Glyn does not get involved in the day, in fact he does his best to stay at the back of the room. His fellow delegates find him negative and obstructive, because he keeps referring to the fact that his absence from work will cause problems for everyone else. The trainer tries to engage his interest, but he is truculent, and makes scathing remarks about the training.

When he completes the evaluation form he states that he has found the day a complete waste of time.

What are the likely effects of Glyn's attitude? What could he have done to make the training event a more positive experience for himself?

_____

_____

_____

_____

We will always find it difficult to learn where we have created obstacles for ourselves – and sometimes we ourselves are the key obstacles that need to be overcome. Glyn needed to agree with his manager and team (and not just with the training department) that the time spent away from the office was essential, even though it may have caused other people immediate problems. Instead of ensuring that everyone knew what he was doing and why, Glyn took his annoyance to the training event and took it out on the people there. This meant that neither he nor they were able to get as much as they could have done from the day. Not a very constructive attitude! His assessment of the training will be worse than useless, because he hasn't taken a self-critical approach to it but just blamed others.

Time and **support** are two of the resources that could have been specified on his development plan.

Development activity needs to be approached as a positive and challenging experience, if we are to become more effective.

Other people cannot make you develop or improve, this is highly personal, and ultimately you need to be aware of the development opportunities that present themselves and make the most of them.

4 Selecting the right form of development

In Session B we looked at the most common forms of development activity, and by now you probably have a reasonable idea of which ones attract you and which don't. You may also have a pretty good idea about which ones are realistic for you. However, to summarize the important points again briefly: when making the decision about which form of activity is right for you, it may be helpful to run through the following factors with your manager or mentor.

■ The best way(s) of achieving your performance objective.
■ The development opportunities currently available.
■ Your preferred learning style(s).
■ A cost-benefit analysis of resources, i.e. looking at the cost of the resources needed in relation to the benefits of achieving the performance objective.
■ Alternative development opportunities, i.e. those outside the development practices you usually consider.

When you have looked at each of these issues, you will be able to fill in the third column on the PDP form (resources).

The final bullet point above may need some explanation. It is important to remember that development can take place in a range of situations, planned or otherwise, and we need to be aware of these as they arise and incorporate them into our plan if possible. It is part of our responsibility for our own development that we take these opportunities, planned or not, where they will contribute to the achievement of our objectives.

5 Reviewing and evaluating development

Reviewing and evaluating your development plan and your performance objectives is an integral part of all development activity. Without this step, we cannot really know how well we're doing.

Many of us do a training course, for example, intending to improve our communication skills, or practise making presentations. But we often return to work full of good intentions, having given the course a positive evaluation, but have then failed to do very much with what we have learned.

Your development plan should prevent this happening, because you should be able to sit down and review the development activity, either on your own or with someone else. Therefore, reviews need to be noted as important dates and times, either in your diary, on a wall chart, or anywhere that is difficult to ignore.

Activities 29 and 30 will help you to ask specific questions of a development activity and its relevance to supporting you in achieving your performance objective(s).

Activity 29 · 2 mins

Ask yourself the following questions in relation to the last development activity that you were involved in.

1   Was the development activity relevant to my performance
    objective(s)?   Yes/No

2   Was there sufficient opportunity and support, back at work,
    to put new ideas into practice?   Yes/No

3   Was the activity itself suited to my learning style?   Yes/No

Did you answer 'no' to any of these three questions? If you did then it is likely that some aspect of the development activity was inappropriate to you and your needs.

Activity 30 · 2 mins

Refer back to Activity 29. Let's assume your response was 'no' to each of the three questions. Now answer the following questions.

1   In what ways was the development activity irrelevant to my performance
    objective(s)?

    _____

    _____

    _____

2   What needed to happen back at work to help me put new ideas into
    practice?

    _____

    _____

    _____

3   What needed to change during the activity to help me work within my
    preferred learning style?

    _____

    _____

    _____

You may have answered that the content of the activity was only partly relevant to your performance objective(s). For example, you might have attended a formal course covering the requirements of giving professional presentations using information technology, when in fact the presentations that you need to give are informal ones, within your own team and using only handouts.

Lack of opportunity to put what's been learned into practice and lack of support back at work following the development activity are often the very things that limit the success of a person's development plan. When listing the resources you will need in your plan, it is essential to include opportunities and support as resources.

Once a full review has been carried out then you may find it necessary to reconsider other development activities that have been included in the development plan. You and your line manager might realize that some planned development activities are not likely to support you in fulfilling your objective. You may decide that other forms of development activity may be more suitable, and your plan will need to be changed to reflect these decisions.

5.1 Evaluating your personal development plan

We can evaluate our plan by how much closer we feel we are to achieving our performance objective. This may be done in a number of ways.

- Through **personal consideration**, making our own assessment of how close we are to achieving the objective.
- By **asking others**, e.g. colleagues, team members. Feedback, as explored earlier, is an essential factor in our development. Ask others to describe where they can see improvements in your performance, also ask for suggestions and ideas for further improvement.
- By using **existing measurement techniques in the workplace**. If your organization has procedures for establishing and monitoring quality, use these to find out where your performance has a direct impact on outcomes. For example, suppose the number of customer complaints is published on a weekly basis, and a development activity is offered to staff in order to reduce the number of complaints. We might reasonably assume that a reduction in the published number of complaints is the result of the effectiveness of the development.

You may be able to think of other methods of evaluation.

62

Look back at Maddi's development plan, and note down which forms of review and evaluation she has listed there.

_____

_____

Now decide which forms of review are relevant in your own case and when these might happen. You will probably need to discuss this with a colleague, your manager or mentor.

You can now fill in the fourth and fifth columns of your own PDP form (method(s) of evaluation and date(s) of review).

> Elsa is a Call Centre Manager. She is responsible for monitoring the calls of six Customer Service Consultants. As part of this monitoring process, she needs to offer both positive and critical feedback on how the consultants deal with customers over the telephone. As Elsa's feedback to her staff has a direct impact on the results of customer satisfaction surveys, this is a key aspect of her work.
>
> In her personal development plan, Elsa identified her main development need as being able to offer this type of feedback – she had tended to avoid doing it in the past. She attended a course and also observed other managers giving feedback to their own staff.
>
> Elsa then made a particular effort to offer individual feedback to each team member, and monitored the customer satisfaction figures immediately afterwards. She was able to see a distinct improvement, especially in the consistently helpful approach adopted by all her staff.
>
> Comments from her staff also helped Elsa to recognize that the development activities she had undertaken have had a direct and positive impact on the performance of all concerned.

Which methods of review and evaluation did Elsa use?

By fully reviewing and evaluating each development activity, and learning from this process, we can judge its effectiveness in helping us to achieve our objectives. Elsa was able to tell how effective her efforts at development had been by looking at the statistics on customer satisfaction and by getting feedback from her own staff.

6 Keeping track

It is important to keep track of your development activities, and one way to do this is by keeping a log of what you do. Keeping a development (or learning) log enables you to:

- compile information for review purposes;
- measure the resources that have been used;
- record types of development activity for future reference.

Professional bodies have various types of membership requirements, and these can involve logging and recording development activity, as part of a continuing professional development strategy. If you belong to a professional organization (or are thinking of becoming a member of one), a development log can provide information to help with your application or with upgrading your membership (e.g. from associate to full membership).

A development log should:

- outline what was involved;
- describe the resources used;
- specify the outcomes (e.g. What can I do differently/better as a result of the activity?);
- consider the effectiveness of the development activity;
- note the time spent on the activity itself.

A development or learning log will be a reliable record of any development activity that you undertake. It can be used to support your application for other jobs, or promotion within your organization, because it shows a logical and comprehensive approach to your own professional development.

The following template is a possible approach to development logging that you might consider using. If you decide to amend the format, make sure that you cover all the detail required, in order to produce a useful and reliable source of information.

DEVELOPMENT ACTIVITY LOG

Type of activity _____

Performance objective that this supports

_____

_____

Briefly outline what was involved, e.g. course attended, article read, etc.

_____

_____

How much did it cost? _____

Were sources of support available? (specify what these were)

_____

_____

Other resources that were needed

_____

_____

How long were you involved in this activity (in hours)? _____

Which skills have you developed as a result of this activity?

_____

_____

What can you now do differently/better that will enable you to achieve your performance objective?

_____

_____

What knowledge have you developed as a result of this activity? How can you apply this knowledge to support the achievement of your performance objective?

_____

_____

What were the positive features of this activity?

_____

_____

What were the negative features of this activity?

_____

_____

Will you use this type of development activity in the future? If yes, why? If no, why not?

_____

_____

Activity 32

15 mins

Think back to the last development activity that you were involved in and complete a development activity log. Make sure that you have included sufficient detail to provide useful and reliable information for future reference.

7 Revising your PDP

The logging and review process will mean that you can eventually make changes to your personal development plan.

Most obviously, your performance objectives will necessarily change, at least they should once you have succeeded in meeting them! (Or, possibly, you may realize that you wrongly identified what you need to be able to do, and need to redefine them.) If it is to remain a useful and current working document, your performance objectives will need to be revised from time to time. You may also need to revise the dates by which the objectives are achieved, if there are any unexpected problems along the way. It is important to remain very clear about the deadlines, otherwise, if there is a hitch, the deadline will just fade away and nothing will have been achieved.

You may find that a development activity needs to be rethought, or dropped, because:

■ similar activity has not been successful or effective;
■ the performance objective has already been achieved.

Resources may need to be reallocated, in order that you can spend more on one form of development than another, simply because you have found that it is the most effective approach.

The method of review may have to change, or the date, because those involved may not be available for some reason, or you may find the type of review you chose was less helpful than expected.

The Work-based assignment at the end of this workbook will give you the chance to revise your own personal development plan.

6.1 Where do you go from here?

You are now approaching the end of this workbook. Through your work so far you should be clearer about what you need to do to become more effective in your job. You may have identified a number of areas where you would like to become more effective, and feel rather daunted by the size of the task. The important thing is that you have already made a start.

In deciding where to go from here, you will probably find it most helpful to start on those areas where you will see the most rapid results, and those are likely to be the top priority development needs you identified in Session B. Achieving visible results as soon as realistically possible is the best way to ensure that you continue to take the time and trouble that professional development inevitably entails.

You may have included career moves in your plans, and if so, what you have learned in this workbook will stand you in good stead as you change direction or move further along your present career path. Whatever the case, we wish you the very best of luck in your efforts.

Self-assessment 3

10 mins

1 List the six main items you need to include on a personal development plan.

_____

_____

_____

_____

_____

_____

2 In order for any planned development to be effective, you need to

_____ _____ for your own attitude towards it.

3   What factors do you need to take into account when selecting a development activity?

_____

_____

_____

_____

_____

4   How can we evaluate effectiveness of any development that we undertake?

_____

_____

_____

5   What does a development, or learning, log enable you to do?

_____

_____

_____

_____

_____

6   How does it differ from a personal development plan?

_____

_____

You will find the answers to these questions on pages 78–9.

8 Summary

- Your attitude to development is an important factor and will affect its success.

- Your personal development is your responsibility, other people cannot make you develop or improve.

- Development opportunities may arise in all sorts of ways, so we need to be aware of these as they come up. It is part of our responsibility for our own development that we take these opportunities where appropriate, and where they will contribute to the achievement of our objectives.

- The factors affecting the decision about suitable development opportunities are: the best way(s) of achieving the defined objective; currently available development opportunities; alternative development opportunities; preferred learning styles; resources.

- Reviewing our development activity is not just a useful thing to do, it is essential if we are ever to develop at all.

- We need to evaluate the effectiveness of the development activity, and also how it helps us to attain our performance objective and fulfil our development need.

- Development takes many different forms and so it is important to keep track of the development activities we have undertaken.

- A development, or learning, log should enable you to:
  - outline what was involved;
  - define resources used;
  - specify the outcomes;
  - consider the effectiveness of the development activity overall;
  - note the time spent on the activity itself.

- Any relevant outcomes from the logging and review process should be incorporated into our personal development plan.

Performance checks

1 Quick quiz

Question 1   What are the **four** key areas of most managerial roles?

Question 2   What are some of the forms and sources of job-related information that you might access?

Question 3   What are the key questions to ask in relation to job activities or tasks?

Question 4   What factors do you need to consider in a PESTLE analysis?

Question 5   What is a SMART objective?

Question 6   Why is support a fundamental resource in planning development?

Question 7   What are the practical uses of a formal development plan?

Question 8   What factors can we take into consideration when identifying development opportunities?

Question 9   How do you evaluate the usefulness of a personal development plan?

Question 10 How will the production of a development or learning log support the personal development planning process?

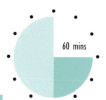

60 mins

2 Workbook assessment

Christine is in charge of the invoicing department of a medium-sized engineering company. She has been in the job for the past three years. At first she was responsible for the performance of a team of three people, but this has expanded to eight people, because of company growth and expansion.

The job was functional, in that she handled a great deal of the invoicing process herself. This has now changed and now the team members handle the whole invoicing process, while she oversees their work. However, recently there have been a number of mistakes, resulting in customer complaints. Christine is aware that she is not comfortable in actually managing the staff concerned, and often takes over some of the invoicing work herself – otherwise she feels she is not doing enough work. Staff have complained to Christine's line manager that they feel unsupported and that by doing their work herself she seems to be criticizing their capability.

Christine has had a performance review with her manager, and these issues have been raised. She now needs to focus on her development, something that she has not done in the past.

Write down your answers to the following questions.

1   How would you define Christine's key responsibilities as a manager?

2   What skills and knowledge does Christine need to develop?

3   What performance objective(s) would you set and agree with Christine?

4   What forms of development would be appropriate in helping to achieve these objectives?

5   Briefly outline the resources that would support these development activities?

Give the reasons behind your thinking. You can make any assumptions about Christine, her team and her work that seem reasonable.

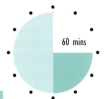

60 mins

3 Work-based assignment

S/NVQ C1.1

The time guide for this assignment gives you an approximate idea of how long it is likely to take you to write up your findings. You will find that you need to spend additional time gathering information, perhaps talking to colleagues as well as your manager, and thinking about the assignment.

Your written response to this assignment may form the basis of useful evidence for your S/NVQ portfolio. It will also help you to manage personal learning and development.

Before you can complete this assignment, you will have had to undertake at least **ONE** of the development activities you listed in your personal development plan.

The assignment is designed to help you demonstrate the following.

- Your ability to take responsibility for meeting your own learning and development needs.
- Your ability to seek feedback on performance.
- Your ability to learn from your mistakes.
- Your ability to change your plans where needed as a result of feedback.
- Your ability to reflect systematically on your own performance and modify it as a result of undertaking personal development activities.
- Your ability to develop yourself to meet the demands of changing situations.
- Your ability to transfer learning from one situation to another.

What you have to do

In this assignment you look at the personal development plan that you developed in Session C in the light of having undertaken at least one of the development activities that it contains. The aim is to evaluate the plan and revise it so that it takes account of the development activity you have been involved in.

The first step is to gather together all the relevant information you need to carry out an evaluation and revision of the plan. This will, or may, include:

- the personal development plan you created in Session C of this workbook;
- copies of the blank PDP form;

- information about the development activity(s), such as evaluation forms or notes;
- any material that you have since been able to produce in the course of doing your job, as a result of doing the activity (e.g. presentation or briefing material);
- information gathered as a result of feedback from colleagues or other relevant people;
- any other material that seems relevant to your situation (e.g. information about future changes produced by your organization or other professional or public bodies, information about other forms of development activity, etc.).

You may also find it useful to refer to some of the other material you have produced elsewhere in this workbook, such as the PESTLE analysis or feedback forms from Session A.

The second step is to arrange a meeting with your line manager, or other relevant person, in order to discuss the plan. They may or may not want or need to see copies of the information you have gathered. The date and time of the meeting will need to be arranged so that all concerned have time to look at the material and assess it beforehand.

The third step is to draw up a written summary of the information you have gathered. Re-read the various documents, and make notes for yourself that assess the following.

- The usefulness or otherwise of the development activity(s) – did it meet your performance objective(s)?
- The response to any material you produced during the course of your work.
- Your colleagues' comments, and any other methods of evaluation used.
- Future plans, in the light of expected changes or new development activities you wish to consider.
- Changes you think are necessary to the PDP (e.g. revising your performance objectives).
- Resources you might need in future.

Next, take all this material to the meeting and discuss it thoroughly with the other person involved. If this is your line manager, only include changes to the PDP that are AGREED between you, that is, those that are approved and have support, and are therefore most likely to happen.

Finally, write up the revised development plan, obtain your line manager's formal approval for it, and keep it where you can easily refer to it again when necessary.

The written summary and revised development plan together need not be more than two or three pages long.

Reflect and review

1 Reflect and review

Now that you have completed your work on *Becoming More Effective* let us review the workbook objectives. The first objective was as follows.

■ You should be better able to analyse and build a sound picture of your current skills, knowledge and personal attributes, using a range of techniques and approaches.

By examining in depth the actual requirements of your job, you will now better understand what you yourself need in order to do the job well. Each job needs the jobholder to possess certain types of skill and knowledge, and to behave appropriately. A detailed personal analysis of the different factors affecting us, now and in the future, can produce a full list of our present weaknesses. When this listing is matched to the requirements of our job we can quickly establish what we need to be able to do.

Ask yourself these questions.

■ Do I really know what my job is about, and what I need in order to do the job well?

■ Do I recognize my present strengths and weaknesses?

The second objective was as follows.

■ You should be better able to undertake a personal training and development needs analysis

By gathering information from different sources, and by using this information in an analytical and practical way, you have begun to determine what you really need by way of development. As things around us change, including your job, you will need to revisit your findings, constantly re-assessing your development needs. You need to regularly ask yourself these questions.

- How are the organisation and its operating environment changing?

- How will current changes, internally and externally, impact on my ability to do the job?

- What strengths do I have that will help me weather and manage these changes?

- How can I prioritize and address any identified weaknesses, in order to weather and manage these changes?

The third objective was as follows.

■ You should be better able to develop and revise your own personal development plan.

A development plan is a practical means of clarifying what you need to do, while identifying how best to achieve this. Through a thorough exploration of performance requirements, usually with your own line manager, you will produce a detailed plan that will illustrate what needs to be done, the types of development that are useful, as well as details of resources needed and the timescales that are required. Ask yourself these questions.

- Is my development planned?

- is my development plan a working document, something that is an integral part of my working life?

The fourth objective was as follows.

■ You should be better able to identify and select appropriate training and development opportunities.

As development can take a number of different forms it is very important to be able to identify those opportunities that are directly relevant to your needs. Specifying what you will be able to do once you have undertaken the development activity, can help you decide which forms of development are most useful. You are also now aware that you like to learn in a particular way, i.e. that you have a preferred learning style. This means that certain forms of development will be more appropriate to you and your personal needs, than will others. The key questions are these.

- What are my performance objectives – what will I be able to do, what will I know, once I have completed the development activity?

- How do I learn, and what development opportunities are suitable to my preferred learning style?

■ Am I overlooking development opportunities because they don't suit my preferred learning style?

The final objective was as follows.

■ You should be better able to evaluate and record the training and development activities that you have been involved in.

Every development plan needs to be revised and amended, so that it remains current and reliable. You revise and amend your plan after evaluating it. This involves considering the effectiveness of the development activities, as well as the direct impact of the development on your performance at work. If your development plan is to be a real working document it needs to change and reflect the realities of your own situation. Evaluation should always involve you in asking these questions.

■ How has the development that I have undertaken improved my performance at work?

■ What do I do and/or know now that I did not do and/or know before the development took place?

■ Was this the most appropriate form of development for my particular situation or need?

2 Action plan

Use this plan to further develop for yourself a course of action you want to take. Make a note in the left-hand column of the issues or problems you want to tackle, and then decide what you intend to do, and make a note in column 2.

The resources you need might include time, materials, information or money. You may need to negotiate for some of them, but they could be something easily acquired, like half an hour of somebody's time, or a chapter of a book. Put whatever you need in column 3. No plan means anything without a timescale, so put a realistic target completion date in column 4.

Finally, describe the outcome you want to achieve as a result of this plan, whether it is for your own benefit or advancement, or a more efficient way of doing things.

Desired outcomes				
	1 Issues	2 Action	3 Resources	4 Target completion
Actual outcomes				

3 Extensions

Extension 1	Book	*The Manual of Learning Styles*
	Author	Peter Honey and Alan Mumford
	Edition	Revised edition 1992
	Publisher	Peter Honey Publications
	ISBN	095 08444 7 0
Extension 2	Book	*Using Your Learning Styles*
	Author	Peter Honey and Alan Mumford
	Edition	1986
	Publisher	Peter Honey Publications
	ISBN	095 08444 38

4 Answers to self-assessment questions

Self-assessment 1 on page 22

1 Job-related information comes in a range of forms and from a variety of SOURCES.

2 Every job is made up of key TASKS and activities

3 In order to be effective we need a combination of skills, KNOWLEDGE and personal attributes.

4 Weaknesses that MUST be addressed quickly are those that will involve job requirements that are fundamental to the overall day-to-day performance of your job.

5 The factors that comprise a PESTLE analysis are: POLITICAL, ECONOMIC, SOCIAL, TECHNOLOGICAL, LEGAL, ENVIRONMENTAL/ECOLOGICAL.

6 It is essential to seek feedback as others often see us differently to the way we see ourselves.

7   We can make sure that feedback is valid and reliable by making sure it comes from a range of sources; from people who are in a position to offer comment and who are going to be honest and constructive.

Self-assessment 2
on page 48

1   **Training** is a planned series of activities with limited objectives that enables the trainees to do something they couldn't do before. **Learning** is how we absorb new information and apply it in practice. **Development** is the process of growth and change that may involve both training and learning.

2   In order to change a weakness into a strength, you need to set yourself clear **performance objectives**.

3   In order to be effective, you need to set yourself performance objectives that are:

- Specific
- Measurable
- Achievable
- Relevant
- Time bound

4

The experiential learning cycle

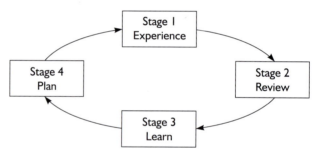

5   The types of development activity you may have mentioned are: training courses and programmes, coaching, mentoring, distance learning, work-based projects, computer-based training, planned or guided reading.

6   You will find a development activity either attractive or unattractive, depending on your **preferred learning style**.

7   The four basic styles of learning are: **activist**, **reflector**, **theorist** and **pragmatist**.

Self-assessment 3
on page 66

1   The main items a personal development plan needs to include are:

- a statement of the development need(s);
- the performance objective(s);
- the date by when the objective needs to be achieved;
- the type of development activity and the resources required;
- the method(s) of evaluation;
- the dates of review.

2 In order for any development activity to be effective, you need to **take responsibility** for your own attitude towards it.

3 Factors you need to take into account when selecting development activities are as follows.

- What is the best way of achieving your performance objective?
- Which forms of development are available in practice?
- What is your preferred learning style?
- Is the activity worth what it will cost? (i.e. Is the objective it meets worth paying that amount for?)
- Are there any alternatives?

4 We can evaluate effectiveness of any development that we undertake through personal consideration; by asking others; and by using existing measurement techniques in the workplace.

5 A development, or learning, log enables you to:

- outline what was involved in the development;
- define resources used;
- specify the outcomes, e.g. what can I do differently/better as a result of the activity;
- consider the effectiveness of the development activity overall;
- note the time spent on the activity itself.

6 A development log describes what happened in practice, while a development plan describes what we want to happen.

6 Answers to the quick quiz

Answer 1 Managing activities and quality, managing financial and physical resources, managing people, yourself and relationships and managing communication and information.

Answer 2 Some of the forms and sources of job-related information that you might access are:

- a job description;
- a person specification;
- completed appraisal or performance review forms;
- an organisation chart – showing the relationship between your job role and others within the company;
- discussions with your line manager, human resource staff, colleagues or others doing the same job as you to find out more.

Answer 3   The key questions to ask in relation to job activities or tasks are as follows.

- What do I need to be able to do?
- What do I need to know?
- What personal attributes do I need to possess?

Answer 4   The factors you need to consider in a PESTLE analysis are as follows.

- **P**olitical
- **E**conomic
- **S**ocial
- **T**echnological
- **L**egal
- **E**nvironmental/ecological

Answer 5   A SMART objective is one that is:

- **S**pecific
- **M**easurable
- **A**chievable
- **R**elevant
- **T**ime bound.

Answer 6   Support is a fundamental resource in planning development because we might need support to put our learning into practice, or change working practices. Support will also help us to be sure we are developing in the right direction, with a chance of achieving our performance objective.

Answer 7   The practical uses of a formal development plan are:

- setting out development needs;
- listing methods of development;
- setting review and completion dates;
- itemising the resources needed to fulfil the defined needs.

Answer 8   The factors we take into consideration when identifying development opportunities include:

- the best way(s) of achieving the defined performance objective;
- the development opportunities currently available;
- preferred learning styles;
- a cost-benefit analysis of resources, i.e. looking at the cost of the resources needed in relation to the benefits of achieving the defined performance objective.
- alternative development opportunities, i.e. outside the usually considered development practices.

Answer 9   We evaluate a personal development plan by: personal consideration, by asking others and by employing existing measurement techniques in the workplace.

Answer 10   The development or learning log helps the personal development planning process by using the information gathered from logging to inform the review and amendment of the personal development plan.

6 Certificate

Completion of this certificate by an authorized person shows that you have worked through all the parts of this workbook and satisfactorily completed the assessments. The certificate provides a record of what you have done that may be used for exemptions or as evidence of prior learning against other nationally certificated qualifications.

Pergamon Flexible Learning and ILM are always keen to refine and improve their products. One of the key sources of information to help this process are people who have just used the product. If you have any information or views, good or bad, please pass these on.

INSTITUTE OF LEADERSHIP & MANAGEMENT
SUPERSERIES

Becoming More Effective

....

has satisfactorily completed this workbook

Name of signatory ....

Position ....

Signature ....

Date ....

Official stamp

Fourth Edition

INSTITUTE OF LEADERSHIP & MANAGEMENT
SUPERSERIES
FOURTH EDITION

To order – phone us direct for prices and availability details
(please quote ISBNs when ordering) on 01865 888190